Children of the Reverie Hour

By Briana Jade Dobson

To those who have touched me greatly in my life.

If it is God's will our paths will cross again.

Table of Contents

Introduction

Section 1: Dream of the Future World

Section 2: Where We Came

Section 3: A Parable or Two for Me and You

Section 4: A Walk of Faith and Trust

Section 5: Trapped As Children

Section 6: Trial By Fire and a Test of Courage

Section 7: Love and Departure

Introduction

As fragile as life can be there is one thing we can always find steadiness in the eye of the storm. At times it feels like our ship will sink. Our hunger to find a new, better world may not be enough to get us to the place God has placed in our minds. The vision of something more. Visions don't just come to us, they've been there since birth and God has given every last one of us enough water or our gift to get through the wilderness to find the promised land. I know this because I've been there and I'm still there, girded with a gift He has given me in hopes to use it as my arrow to the post.

My poems were inspired by not just some flash of light, but by God. He reached out his hand to me at a time in my life where I thought I was going to lose myself. When I first entered my teenage years, it was a change. I didn't understand. I didn't know what was wrong with me. I couldn't find myself and I didn't want to be in this life anymore since I didn't know my direction. A bow and arrow without a target is unsteady and can go anywhere. So God heard my cry and I found my escape and I opened a door to another realm.

It is in these times that He taught me. Trained me, to cope with anger, pain, sadness, happiness, love, excitement, and so many other things. I became like a newly born fawn in May with my newly discovered gift. Other inspirations were from people. Such as my family, other adults, kids I saw around me, kings and apostles in the Bible, and an artist named Efisio Cross. All these people helped me create this bow that I now use to aim where my arrows go. I hope to accomplish helping you better understand yourself and to hopefully make you not want to give up on life and to hopefully let you know that you're not alone in this world, but that there are others like you standing in a field of haziness with a bow and arrow searching for a target.

Dream of the Future World

Section 1

The Fantasy Garden

Roaring and bellowing as the waterfall falls upon stones and rocks.

Light as a feather and swift as an Apodidae is the dragonfly.

Clay and stone are the stairs that were created still and non-perishable.

Blossoming and blooming with life the flowers shall seem to never vanish.

Bringing the warm breeze from the south and the west, the mouth of the ocean blows.

Shining bright and bringing life to whatever it touches, the sun shall during the day.

Awakening and things that go bump in the night shall the moon bring alive.

Thundering and crackling the horses roam freely and willingly.

Sprouting and growing the Earth bringeth fruit of every kind.

Rustling and blowing either direction, the wind blows the trees shall go.

Flowing and conquering anything in its path the river has a mind of its own.

Open that doorway to the imagination of a child and there shall you find your fantasy garden.

A Dream Of Imagination

If the world were free of sickness and Illness.

    It would be a dream of imagination.

If the world were free of war and disagreements.

    It would be a dream of imagination.

If the world were free from sin and disobedience.

    It would be a dream of imagination.

If the world were free of anger and jealousy.

It would be a dream of imagination.

If the world were free of hunger and thirst.

It would be a dream of imagination.

If the world were free of blindness and none hear

It would be a dream of imagination.

If the world were free of sorrow and sadness.

It would be a dream of imagination.

If the world were innocent as a child and trusted God.

It would be a dream of imagination.

If the world were free of so many religions and they joined one.

It would be a dream of imagination.

If the world were free from all the plagues and all sin it would be a dream of imagination.

Note: We all wish this were true of course its not, but if it were true would God have had to send his only begotten son to die for us? Would there be a life after this life? Would we be living on this earth forever? Ask yourself these questions, would I be the same person I am today If things were different?

The Night Song

Come now my children, I'll show thee the way.

And take thee to a land of enchantment.

Open thy doors now and join me this night.

Sing on my children, sing me a tune.

Sing now my children, sing the night song to awaken the creatures of the night.

Oh, come now my children bring me my song.

Sing me my song tis night and every night to awaken the creatures of the night.

Til the darkness disappears you'll sing me this song.

Oh, now ye children follow me to come and rest in the enchanted place.

Open my portal and we shall disappear.

Open, open I say at the song of my mouth.

Come now my children and let us rest till the next night.

Then shall we awaken and have a fest.

Where We Came

Section 2

Would I Be the Same

If circumstances were better or worse.

Would I be the same?

If I were a richer or poorer person.

Would I be the same?

If I had a perfect or bad family.

Would I be the same?

If I were a free person instead of a prisoner.

Would I be the same?

If I were famous instead of unknown.

Would I be the same?

If I were in school instead of at home.

Would I be the same?

If I were a failure instead of a great success.

Would I be the same?

If I were any weaker instead of strong.

Would I be the same?

If anything in this world were any different would I be the same?

Note: Different things affect the way we live and act. Sometimes we say, 'I wish circumstances were worse or better,' but ask yourself this. "Would I be the same?" The answer is 'no,' you would not be the same if circumstances were different. Because the way we live and the circumstances God puts us into are a;; going according to His perfect plan. Not our plan, but His. So you may not really want to change your circumstances for better or worse, because you might just make it so you can't do something else.

Is It Worth It

        Is this change worth the pain that I may gain?   Is it worth it?   Is it worth falling or stumbling that I may walk?

                                        Is it
worth it?
            Is something worth losing so that I may
            gain more of something else?
                                        Is it
worth it?
            Is falling worth learning even
            though I failed?
                                        Is it
worth it?
            Is waiting worth waiting for if
            you're not sure what it is?
                                        Is it
worth it?
            Is leaving behind worth leaving if I
            don't know what is ahead?
                                        Is it
worth it?
            Is family worth having if
            something was to happen?
                                        Is it
worth it?
            Is love worth having if it means
            losing sometimes connections?

                    Is it worth
it?
            Is working worth working if I
have worries back at home?
                        Is it worth
it?
    Is sharing something worth sharing if there is
nothing in return for you?
                        Is it worth
it?
                    Is anything worth
            anything?

Note: I say this is not to confuse you, but to ask a question, is anything worth anything. If you are wondering what the answer is, I will tell you. If you have been asking yourself this day in and day out. The answer is that everything is worth everything in the end because everything is a living experience. Even if it is painful, even if you are unsure, even if you fail, all things work together for good to those that love God, to those who are called to

His perfect plan and purpose. So it is all worth it in the end.

What is the Purpose

The river flows and breaketh through rocks and stones making another way to flow each time it passes the same way.

What is the purpose?

Geysers shoot hot water out of their mouths.

What is the purpose?

A fire is started and burns and devourers everything in its path.

What is the purpose?

The beavers build their dam in the way of the river creating a lake.

What is the purpose?

Footprints along the beach in the sand are washed every time the tide comes in.

What is the purpose?

The moon goes down, the sun comes up, the sun goes down and the moon comes up.
What is the purpose?
Water on the ground turns into vapor creating clouds.
What is the purpose?
You may run into mean or nice people.
What is the purpose?
The wind blows cold and hot air into different places.
What is the purpose?
The tree is still and its leaves can be blown any way.
What is the purpose?
What is the purpose of everything in this world?
What is the purpose?

Note: You may ask yourself, what is the purpose for this and that, but have you figured out your purpose in this world? If not, you should pray to God and ask Him, what is your purpose on this earth. Everything in this world has a purpose, whether big or small, tall or short everything has a purpose. We may not always know what something's purpose is all the time or right off.

Paint My World

Paint my world with love and happiness.
Paint my world with many colors.
Paint my world with empathy and peace.
Paint my world with joy instead of sorrow.
Paint my world with beauty and brilliance.
Paint my world with kindness and patience.
Paint my world with brightness everywhere.
Paint my world with goodness and fruitfulness.
Paint my world with faith and hope.
Paint my world with fellowship between friends and family.
Paint my world with Jesus and God always with us.
Paint my world with lavender-purple flowers.
Paint my world with crimson red roses.
Paint my world with natural amazements.
Paint my world with imagination and fantasy.
Paint my world with anything I think of.

Note: You can paint your world with anything you want, this is your world to paint. You can paint your world with happiness or sadness. It's all the way in which you look at this world. If you see darkness everywhere that's what you paint, if you see beauty everywhere that's what you paint. This is your world to paint, not mine or anyone else's because we can't paint your world for you. So whatever you see, that's what you paint.

If Things Could Change

What if the sky was green and the grass was blue and everything around you was different?
If things could change, what would you choose?
What if the life you live as someone else's and theirs yours and everyone around you different?
If things could change, what would you choose?
What if the world we live in was all desert and the land was all dry and everything around you was different?
If things could change, what would you choose?
What if your time was up in this world and another time began at that same time and everything around you was different?

If things could change, what would you choose?
What if everything was turned upside down and gravity disappeared and everything around you was different?

If things could change, what would you choose?
What if an apple turned into an orange and the orange an apple and everything around you was different?

If things could change, what would you choose?
What if the sun had no light of its own and the moon gave the sunlight and everything around you was different?

If things could change, what would you choose?
What if the day was night and the night was day and everything around you was different?

If things could change, what would you choose?
What if the family you have could be perfect and another family not and everything around you was different?

If things could change, what would you choose?

What if you could bring back your old fun past time memories of the past and live in the future and everything around you was different?

If things could change, what would you choose?

What if you could live a better way than you live now or what if you could live the same as you do and everything around you was different?

If things could change, what would you choose?

What if seas were land and the land was the sea and everything around you was different?

If things could change, what would you choose?

What if you could be someone famous and someone who is common and everything around you was different?

If things could change, what would you choose? **Note:** We always can find something to complain about. My hair is too short or my hair is too long. Or today is too hot or today's too cold. We can easily find something to complain about, you almost never hear. God gave me a life and God gave me each and every day to enjoy and find something pleasurable about it and for us to find His grace that he gave us another day. Sometimes we think if things were this way, they would be better, but ask ourselves. How will this make Him feel for wanting to change this or change what He's created? Do you really want to change what God has in mind or instore for your life? Would you really choose to change what God hath created, if you could? Ask yourself this question each time you think that you want to change something.

Somewhere Out There

Somewhere out there in the world my life began, someone or something called me on the inside, the trees in the forest blew back and forth in the breeze as though they were calling for someone.

Somewhere out there, across the ridges and rivers in the green forests and woodland valleys, my destiny awaits.

Somewhere out there, there are places and things yet to be discovered alongside the dirt roads and paths.

Somewhere out there, there is a rock that stands alone and still, though the waves crash upon it, it can not be broken.

Somewhere out there, across the treacherous waters and lands, there will be a way to cross.

Somewhere out there, through the golden wheat fields, through the shining sun, a treasure shall be found.

Somewhere out there across the snow lands and through the cold icy trees, there is something that was lost.

Somewhere out there, above the impossible and beyond the possible, there will be limits on the inside and outside for mankind, whatever those limits are they will stop anyone who dares to go past or over.

Somewhere out there, over the walls of stone and into the lands of forbidden, there will be places that shall not be reached.

Somewhere out there, through the darkness and into the deep, there will be a light to guide our ways.

Somewhere out there, there are places beyond the dreams and places that have never been explored and are left to be that way forever.

Somewhere out there, through the constant waves and through the land arches and gateways, we will find ourselves.

Somewhere out there, through the lavender-purple flowers and plants, through the misty grasses, shadows shall be seen in the distance.

Somewhere out there, through cold and merciless woods, near a river of crystal clear, near a log reaching over the river and a small patch of flowers above it, there it shall be known as home.

Somewhere out there where the sun stretches over the land the darkness has vanished. Somewhere out there above the clouds and into the heavens the answer to why I'm here is out there.

Somewhere out there through the thick mist and the rushing waters, the question why, where, when, how is asked over and over.

Somewhere out there, along those shores and beaches the mind wanders about what is out there.

Somewhere out there, through the dirt paths and roads, the dust is made clear for those to see.

Somewhere out there, through the endless wilderness and over the mountains, hope is lost and hope is gained.

Somewhere out there, through the breathtaking falls and islands, the heart shall be found.

Somewhere out there, through the cold and unforgiving snow, many shall turn back and shall be forsaken.

Somewhere out there, through the gorges and rivers, there shall be some things kept and unseen.

Somewhere out there, through the vast and beautiful fields, something calls us home.

Somewhere out there, through the cosmos and universe, the limits will always want to be tested.

Somewhere out there, through the amazements and sights, the question of why will be asked.

Somewhere out there, through everything and every place, there shall always be wonder, curiosity, challenges beyond your imagination, but the questions are many and the answers are sometimes not found to them.

Nothing Stays the Same

The birds come and go as the season's change.

Nothing stays the same.

The people build and they tear down.

Nothing stays the same.

Children grow and parents grow old.

Nothing stays the same.

The old king's rule then it is time for the kings to rule.

Nothing stays the same.

There's a beginning and an end for everything and everyone.

Nothing stays the same.

The seasons change and it is cold then hot.

Nothing stays the same.

The mind may change and the heart is the same.

Nothing stays the same.

Note: Everything changes after a certain period of time, only God's word and love doesn't change. The only thing that may change is your interpretation of the bible and your love may become even stronger and better.

Things We Were Once Sure Of

That we may forever remain the same happy people.

    Things we were once sure of have now become a question.

That nothing could separate or harm our relationship.

    Things we were once sure of have now become a question.

That our family would remain together until a day of temptation struck.

    Things we were once sure of have now become a question.

That we could support each other through any decision.

    Things we were once sure of have now become a question.

That our trust was stable and so was our hope and faith.

    Things we were once sure of have now become a question.

That we knew each other, better than anyone else till after that day came.

    Things we were once sure of have now become a question.

That our friendship was more sound than a stone house.

    Things we were once sure of have now become a question.

Note: Throughout everything in this life that I was once sure of was brought to question when the time of trials by fire and hail rained upon this desolate place we call our home. The things that we were sure of, our families, our friends, companions, and even sometimes our beliefs are sometimes brought to question and we are no longer sure if we'll or things will come through in the future.

A Parable or Two for Me and You

Section 3

The Tale of The Seed Sowers

There were once two sowers. One was named Jaret Mill and the other Daren Mick. Each man sowed their own seeds and expected something good back. One spring morning the two men went outside to start their crops. Jaret planted wheat hoping for something good to come back after his hard work, as for Daren he went out and only planted tares.

He expected something good to come back. At the end of Summer Jaret went out and had land full of beautiful golden wheat, as for Daren he had nothing but tare's on his land. And on that same day, Daren walked over to Jerets farm, saying unto Jaret. "Why do ye have a land of golden wheat and I only have a land full of tares?"

And Jaret said unto him. "Do ye plant only tares and you expect wheat back. Wherefore why doth thou envy me? Did I plant the tares on your land?"

And Daren answered him, saying. "No."

"You planteth wheat and I plant tare's," Jaret said, "yea, ye planteth tare's ye expect wheat to come back. Whatever ye plant shall come back to you."

Daren said, "my dear friend how foolish have I been to think that I shall plant tares and get back wheat. My friend forgive me for all the trouble that I've caused you."

Note: When we plant spiritual seeds in life, we can expect to get the same thing which we have planted back, just like in the story the man that planted wheat got wheat back, and as for the man that planted tares got tares back. So whatever you plant, good or bad, you're going to get something back, the good thing is when you admit that you were wrong to God he will help you through the storm.

The Tale of The Harvest

There was once a farmer named Mark Jack and he knew when Spring came it would be time for him to tend to the ground. Now the time was right and he went outside. He harnessed his oxen and got started with turning the dirt over with his plow. Afterwards, he went back into the barn and took a sack of seeds. He tossed the seeds roundabout himself, some flew and went into the stream and others fell on the soil.

Afterward, he covered all the seeds with dirt and then watered them. The plants seemed to grow well for the most part, but the farmer checked on them every day. Watering and making sure there were no weeds trying to take over, but when the farmer had to weed his plants it didn't seem to be a delightful thing for the plants. But every time he did so, the plants grew much better. Now Autumn had come and it was time for the farmer to harvest his plants. It was a hard day's work that day and after he separated the wheat from the tares. When he was through, the farmer was filled with great joy of having such a wonderful harvest.

Note: In this tale, the farmer represents God and how we are His harvest. God is the good farmer, who tends to his plants, which is us. He weeds us so we can produce more fruit. He waters us so that we may grow and of all. He loves us and when he calls you home, he has harvested you just like the farmer in the story.

The Tale of The Messenger's Message

There was once a messenger, who went any and everywhere to give a message to everyone. Whether it was good or bad. Special or not special. It was his duty to make sure everyone received their message. One day as he was giving messages to everyone, he met a person named John Dile. Now John Dile, a man of great wisdom in the sight of man said unto the messenger. "I'm a man of wisdom and have no need for a messenger."

And with those words, he sent the messenger away. The second house the messenger walked to was owned by a man named Stevenson James. Being a man of no need of anything said unto the messenger. "That message that ye tell me about is not true for there is no such thing that can happen unto me."

And he sent the messenger away. The messenger walked down the street, hoping the next time he would find a person wiser in heart and an ear to hear. The messenger stopped by the last house on the block. It was not as great as the houses he had been to. He knocked on the door and he told the man the message and the man hearkened unto the messenger's words and abandoned the block. Now ten days later the two men, who didn't listen, lost both their houses and possessions. Now as for the man that listened to the messenger, he had a nice hotel and had replaced all the possessions he had lost.

Note: The messenger represents God's messengers and when God sends these messengers to speak his messages. If we are wise, we will listen to God's messengers instead of sending them away and trying to avoid the message. For it is written, "He that hath an ear, let him hear," (Rev 2:29).

A Walk of Faith and Trust

Section 4

The Only One Standing

Laughing and mocking the Bible. Am I the only one standing?

Glaring and staring at believers. Am I the only one standing?

Friends and family leaving me alone, because I believe. Am I the only one standing?

Everyone turns away from me, for I am a disgrace unto them. Am I the only one standing?

Believing and saying that Jesus isn't real. Am I the only one standing?

No one talks, no one speaks to me. Am I the only one standing?

People plotting and scheming to eliminate me and others. Am I the only one standing?

People shouting out windows at me. Am I the only one standing?

Whispering and backbiting at many people, who believe. Am I the only one standing?

They bring bad reports on people, who believe. Am I the only one standing?

A mob of angry people compasses me about. Am I the only one standing?

They say "looks like the only one standing for the Bible and look at all of us."

Terrified and shaken am I because it seems I am the only one standing.

Tears of sorrow do I have because it seems I am the only one standing.

Is it true that I am the only one standing for Jesus Christ and the Bible?

Then suddenly, the people disappeared and there I was standing, not alone but I was surrounded by a spiritual army. And Jesus took my hand and said. "Be not afraid, for it is I, Jesus Christ, whom ye believed in. Ye are never the only one standing by yourself for I am always there, even in the midst of thy troubles. Now it is time for me to go home." And that dark world disappeared and there I was the only one standing, but not hurt or in pain. But at the right hand of God with his son.

Note: When you believe in Jesus so much and your faith is so strong, you seem to be the only one standing for Jesus Christ in this world. But you are not the only one standing, because with Christ and God on our side we are in the majority since he is the one above everyone and thing in this world.

They search, but shall not find.

They talk, but they can't hear.

They see but are still yet blind.

They grow but are still children.

They acquire but lose even more.

   They stand but are yet broken.

They obey but are still in rebellion.

They rise but are fallen.

They bless but are yet cursed.

They knock but strike with their heart.

They are wise but are yet foolish.

They say love but hate inside.

They bring peace but yet war.

They bring up, but they yet tear down.

They hurt no one, but they bite with their tongue.

They smile with their mouth but frown with their heart.

Note: Though they hurt you not. They touch you not. They yet harm you with many of their actions and words. Sometimes the most hurtful things that happen are when they do the things unseen to the heart.

The First Star in the Sky

Till the sunshine, ye shall give us our light.

Yea, till the sun shines, ye shall give us our light.

Shine on my star shine, shine, shine.

Yea, shine on my star shine, shine, shine.

Shine before the moon comes up.

Yea, shine before the moon comes up.

Shine through the darkness of the sky.

Yea, shine through the darkness of the sky.

Shine brighter.

Yea, shine brighter.

Let your light shine through and through this dark world.

Yea, let your light shine through and through this dark world.

Oh when ye shine your light, ye light up the night.

Yea, oh when ye shine your light, ye light up the night.

The first star are thee and ye shall always be.

Yea, the first star are thee and ye shall always be.

The first star in the sky I look for.

Yea, the first star in the sky I look for.

Oh, ye bright star. Oh, ye bright star.

Let your light shine so that they may know that ye are there.

Oh let it shine. Yea, let it shine.

Jesus is My...

Jesus is my salvation.

Jesus is my deliverance.

Jesus is my all and all.

Jesus is my great intercessor.

Jesus is my hope.

Jesus is my savior.

Jesus is my all and all.

Jesus is my best friend.

Jesus is my contact with God.

Jesus is my family.

Jesus is my Lord.

Jesus is my King.

Jesus is my all and all.

Jesus is my Light.

Jesus is my joy.

Jesus is my peace.

Jesus is my all and all.

Jesus is my Holy One.

Jesus is my fellowship.

Jesus is my everything and I want nothing more than more of Him.

Note: Jesus is really everything you ever wanted and he is everything unto us.

Time For God

There is time to rest and time to awaken.

But is there time for God?

There is time to teach and a time to learn.

But is there time for God?

There is a time to fail and a time to triumph.

But is there time for God?

There is a time to eat and a time to exercise.

But is there time for God?

There is a time to play and a time to work.

But is there time for God?

There is a time to rain and a time to shine.

But is there time for God?

There is a time to plant and a time to harvest.

But is there time for God?

There is a time to laugh and a time to mourn.

But is there time for God?

There is a time to gather and a time to scatter.

But is there time for God?

There is usually always a time for everything else.

But what about God?

Note: There is time for everything else in this life, except for God? Why is this? Do you ask yourself this question each day, why don't you talk with Him? After all, you always have time for everything else. That's it. You are so busy with so many things and jobs, you don't think you have the time for God. But does God really say how long you have to talk to Him in the Bible, or is it just us, who think it has to be something long with Him? Now sometimes you want to have something along with him. But if you can't seem to have enough time just say a few verses, at least you acknowledge he is still there and that you still think about Him.

Blessed Be the Name of God

Blessed be the name of God, for His miracles.

Blessed be the name of God, for His beautiful Earth.

Blessed be the name of God, for flowers and lilies of the field.

Blessed be the name of God, for the gifts He has given us.

Blessed be the name of God, for all His blessings.

Blessed be the name of God, for we have been saved.

Blessed be the name of God, for His son Jesus Christ.

Blessed be the name of God, for the season of rest.

Blessed be the name of God, for heaven, which he hath created.

Blessed be the name of God, for His mercy and grace.

Blessed be the name of God, for Christ our salvation.

Blessed be the name of God, for Christ our deliverance.

Blessed be the name of God, for Christ our righteous.

Blessed be the name of God, for His magnificent wonders.

Blessed be the name of God, for His promises to reward all who seek Him.

I Am Righteous In the Name of Jesus, I am Righteous

Praise God. Praise God. Jesus paid the price for me at that cross and now I am righteous. I am righteous. In the name of Jesus, I am righteous, in that precious name I am righteous.

Though I may have sinned in the past, present, and future I am righteous. I am righteous. In the name of Jesus, I am righteous, in that precious name I am righteous.

Though I was once not righteous in myself now I am righteous. I am righteous. In the name of Jesus, I am righteous, in that precious name I am righteous.

Though I may not be perfect, I am righteous. I am righteous. In the name of Jesus, I am righteous, in that precious name I am righteous.

Though accusers surround me like fire, I am righteous even if they say I am not, I am righteous. I am righteous. In the name of Jesus, I am righteous, in that precious name I am righteous.

Though people say you are not righteous, I am righteous. I am righteous. I am righteous. Yes, In the name of Jesus I am righteous, in that precious name I am righteous.

Note: If you believe in Jesus you are righteous in Him. Not in yourself, but in Him are you are righteous.

Made in the Image God

I may be different or weird in the sight of man.

But I am beautiful because I am made in the image of God.

I may be short or too tall in the sight of man.

But I am beautiful because I am made in the image of God.

I may not have an arm or a leg in the sight of man.

But I am beautiful because I am made in the image of God.

I may be a nobody or nothing in the sight of man.

But I am someone and something because I am made in the image of God.

Note: Everyone who was created in the image of God is beautiful or special in God's eyes because he created us and he created the world and everything in it. So if he made us in his image, we have no excuse, but to be special or beautiful.

Choosing Your Path

If your path is the path with stones, take it.

So should I say, you shouldn't take that path. No.

For this is your path to take.

If your path is a path with boulders, take it.

So should I say, that's a terrible choice to make? No.

For this is your path to take.

If your path is the path with mud, take it.

So should I say, that's a dirty way to take? No.

For this is your path to take.

Note: You should never judge a person's path. For if it works for, who are we to judge and criticize that person?

I Shall Rise Up with Jesus

Someday at my own time.

I shall rise up with Jesus.

I shall rise from the ashes like a phoenix.

I shall rise up with Jesus.

Someday I shall be up there in heaven.

I shall rise up with Jesus.

And I shall rise up and praise God.

I shall rise up with Jesus.

That special day shall come as a thief in the night.

And I shall rise up with Jesus to heaven.

Note: When you think of a phoenix, you often think of the beautiful fiery bird. But what did this phoenix look like before it changed into this lovely bird? It was not such a charming bird at first, then it transformed into this bird of fire. Same with us, we may not think we are beautiful, but we look just as bad or worse than the phoenix. Then that special say all who believe in God shall rise up like a phoenix and go to heaven and be transformed into something far better than the thing we left on Earth.

Laid Down his Life

He laid down his life for our sin.

Laid down his life, his precious life.

He laid down his life though we were yet against him.

Laid down his life, his precious life.

He laid down his life for God's love for us.

Laid down his life, his precious life.

He laid down his life for our everlasting life.

Laid down his life, his precious life.

He laid down his life for contact between God and man.

Laid down his life, his precious life.

He laid down his life so we might have believed.

Laid down his life, his precious life.

He laid down his life so we might have faith.

Laid down his life, his precious life.

He laid down his life to redeem us.

Laid down his life, his precious life.

He laid down his life for us sinners with no worth.

Laid down his life, his precious life.

He laid down his life to give us eternal and forever life.

Laid down his life, his precious life.

Note: If Jesus was willing to lay down his life for us sinners, surely we sinners can lay down our lives sometimes for one another if the son of God could. When He laid down His life, he was separated from God and He had been in contact with God all his life and had us mocking Him, and yet He laid down his life for us.

Follow Me

I ran to the river to fetch water, but it was dry.

Then Jesus took my hand and said follow me for I will lead thee to rivers of life.

I looked inside my cabinets, but there was no bread.

Then Jesus took my hand and said follow me for I will give thee the bread of life.

I went to the garden in search of shade, but there were no trees.

Then Jesus took my hand and said come I will lead thee to the tree of life.

I looked to the sky, but there was no sunlight or light.

Then Jesus took my hand again and said.

"Follow me for I will lead you to the light of the world.

Then I said unto him. "Where is the river of life? Where is the bread of life? Where is the tree of life? And where is the light of the world?"

And Jesus said again. "I am the river of life. I am the bread of life. I am the tree of life. I am the light of the world, which will shine in thee and I am the only begotten son of God. The lamb in which they sacrificed was a representation of my coming. Now do ye understand?"

And I answered, saying. "I understand Lord."

And I walked with Jesus for the rest of my days.

Note: Do you know who Jesus is? You might have heard of him, but do you really know who he is?

Yet One Will...

Many may fall, many stumble in the darkness.

Yet one will stand, one will walk in the light.

The world may head for destruction and chaos.

Yet one will be saved, one will be given life forever.

Though there are many fake ones in the church.

Yet one will be real, one will hear God.

Though there are many tricksters and black widow spiders.

Yet one will be honest, one shall be an angel of light.

Though there are many wolves and snares.

Yet one will be delivered, one will be a sheep out of danger.

Though there are many vampires, who seek out that life.

Yet one will be with God, one will shine their light.

Though there are many great men of valor that stand in the way.

Yet one will not fear, one will pass through them with God.

Though there are few true believers and many skeptics.

Yet one will truly believe, one will not be skeptical of God.

Note: There is always one that will stand for what's right, even when everyone else doesn't. There can be great consequences, but they do not care because they know God is proud of them. For what's right and not doing what is wrong just because everyone else does.

Fellowship

Through fellowship, we talk and speak what's on our minds.

Through fellowship, we join each other at ceremonies.

But while you are learning what true fellowship is, you may sometimes lose fellowship with family and friends over a small disagreement.

Fellowship. Fellowship. Fellowship, my child.

Through fellowship, we enjoy each other's laughter, songs, memories, and stories.

Through fellowship, we can regain contact with one another.

But while you are learning true fellowship, you may always think you're supposed to be the one to speak or teach or something, but that is not so.

    Fellowship. Fellowship. Fellowship, my child.

Through fellowship, we make great relationships with one another.

Through fellowship, we make some of the best and trusted friends.

But while you are learning true fellowship you may often think that one person's your friend just because he or she tells you what you want to hear.

    Fellowship. Fellowship. Fellowship, my child.

    True fellowship is when we all get together and have dinner and spend time with one another. Fellowship doesn't have to be boring or just about one person and what they have to say, it's about the whole church and everyone hearing what everyone has to say. Including children.

Well said, my child. You understand the meaning of fellowship.

Note: Many people think fellowship is all about one person and what that person has to say or do. But that is not true. True fellowship is when we get together and listen to everyone and everyone has to say because God might use someone else to speak a message, including children and teenagers. Adults sometimes think all children and teenagers have no clue what they're talking about. Well, those children and teenagers right there might have had something important to tell, but just because he or she is a child or teen doesn't mean they have something silly to say.

Life

There is a life beyond your imagination

There is something more than the visible.

Life my child, true life is what makes you alive.

There is something great that you can live right on this earth.

There is something that only you can make on this Earth.

You can create a relationship between you and God.

Life my child, true life is what makes you alive.

There is a feeling you can't explain with others, but it's a good feeling.

There is a way you can feel completely secure and safe.

Life my child, true life is what makes you alive.

Life is a Gift

The sun rises, the sunsets.

Life is a gift.

The fresh water that flows down the falls.

Life is a gift.

The rain that falls and the rainbow that shines across the sky.

Life is a gift.

Someone goes out of the world and someone comes in.

Life is a gift.

The breeze that blows through the trees and bushes.

Life is a gift.

The sun shines day and the moon at night.

Life is a gift.

The shelter keeps warm and the fire burns.

Life is a gift.

We sing, we pray because we know that life is a gift.

And the gift is given only once.

Patience

Through patience works love.

Through patience works empathy.

But also while you're building patience, anger cometh.

Patience. Patience. Patience, my child.

Through patience, miracles

Through patience.

There Am I

There am I standing before judgment, whether I made the mark.

There am I praising God because I made it.

There am I riding in a golden carriage polished and clean.

There am I crowned with a crown of most precious stones.

There am I clothed in a golden robe.

There am I holding a key made of golden brass.

There am I entering the pearly gates.

There am I walking in the streets of gold.

There am I walking through a mansion God created for me.

There am I at peace and harmony.

There am I singing and praising the Lord God.

There am I thanking God that the planet I lived on was not the only destination.

Note: God has created a special place for all his children and all who trust and believe in Him.

Born- Yet a Stranger

Tired and weary, not knowing where to go.

Born, yet a stranger.

Having sight, but cannot see.

Born, yet a stranger.

Unknown to the world and the coming unknown.

Born, yet a stranger.

Unseen and unheard of in the physical.

Born, yet a stranger.

Born and given the breath of life b God.

Born, yet a stranger.

A little pillar. A little prince indeed without a crown that would someday be bestowed upon his head. At one point shame, but someday a gift of glory. Although he was born, yet a stranger, he will someday be born, yet a king.

The Heavenly Bells

I heard the heavenly bells and someone came into the world.

I heard the heavenly bells and someone went out of the world.

I heard the heavenly bells and said "did anyone hear that?"

They all answered and said "no."

I heard the heavenly bells and heard singing and praising.

I heard the heavenly bells and saw an angel.

And he said, "Come up and out of that old body."

I heard the heavenly bells and there I was ascending above, only to look back and see that old body resting in a chair.

I Shall Gain in Heaven

If I shall lose a father or mother on Earth.

Whatever I shall lose on Earth I shall gain in heaven.

If I lose connection with my family and friends.

Whatever I shall lose on Earth I shall gain in heaven.

If I lose the whole world and everyone in it.

Whatever I shall lose on Earth I shall gain in heaven.

If I shall lose my house and my belongings.

Whatever I shall lose on Earth I shall gain in heaven.

If I shall lose an arm or leg.

Whatever I shall lose on Earth I shall gain in heaven.

If I lose my bike or my car.

Whatever I shall lose on Earth I shall gain in heaven.

If I am to lose anything in this life I know that whatever I shall lose on Earth, God is going to restore it more than tenfold.

Note: There is no need to worry, no need to stress for God will take care of all your needs. God hears your cry each day. He hears your needs and you can count on that God is going to help you through. He is going to make sure you gain more in heaven. If you have been mistreated or have been hurt for standing on God's word, you know that God will make it so you gain more in heaven. You will gain more of Him.

One Meeting

One meeting with the right person can go a long way.

At any time God could send someone to change your life.

But how can it?

One meeting with the right person can change your life forever.

Just the presence of a certain person at the right time can change you.

But how can it?

One meeting with the right person can change your life forever.

Just one moment with the right person can change a life.

But how can it?

One meeting with the right person can change your life forever.

Just a short walk and conversation can change a life.

But how can it?

One meeting with the right person can change your life forever.

Just a smile or just the happiness they have can change a life.

But how can it?

One meeting with the right person can change your life forever.

Just an interaction, the time that you gave can change a life.

But how can it?

One meeting with the right person can change your life forever.

Just one meeting in a whole lifetime can change a life forever.

Note: The reason one meeting can be so powerful to a certain person in need of help and you come along and do or say the right thing at the right time can give them hope. And that hope can last through a lifetime. That hope that this world can have something good come out of it. The hope that there are people that still care and help and will take time to talk or interact. The spirit you bring of God, that they can just feel as you talk to them can change their life forever. No matter how long or short, you made an impression on them. An impression of hope that there are still some good out there.

Blessed

Blessed are the people who believe.

Blessed are the people that sing and praise God.

But sometimes you may not feel blessed or feel like praising God.

Blessed. Blessed. Blessed are ye, my child.

Blessed are the poor.

Blessed are the meek.

But sometimes you don't feel blessed because you are on the streets without money.

Blessed. Blessed. Blessed are ye, my child.

Blessed are the peacemakers.

Blessed are the faithful.

But sometimes you may not feel blessed or feel like making peace because you may have an argument.

Blessed. Blessed. Blessed are ye, my child.

Blessed are all the believers in you, oh Lord.

Well said, my child.

Note: God has many blessed children, but they are usually hard to find because most of the time the ones who make a lot of noise and say that they are a blessed child of God may not be what they say they are or they could be an immature child of God.

Faith

Through faith, belief, and trust.

Through faith, love, and kindness.

But also while you are growing in faith, you may not fully believe that God hears you.

Faith. Faith. Faith, my child. True faith.

Through faith, perseverance, and strength.

Through faith, spiritual discernment.

But also while you are growing in faith you may often be discouraged.

Faith. Faith. Faith, my child. True faith.

Through faith, you hear God calling you.

Through faith, you find your purpose in God's kingdom.

But also while you are growing in faith, you may sometimes ignore God calling you to your purpose.

Faith. Faith. Faith, my child. True faith.

Through faith, trials, and burnings are very great.

Through faith, patience, and peace.

But also while you are growing in faith, it may sometimes be easy to lose patience.

Faith. Faith. Faith, my child. True faith.

Through faith, you don't look upon things below, but above.

Through faith, even in your darkest hour you know there is God.

Well said, my child.

Note: Faith is something that we can discern God's presence and his kingdom with. Faith also helps us during the hardest and darkest hours. It is that faith that we have that gets us through those hard times. The more faith grows, the stronger we get and you pay less and less attention to the things that are going on around you.

Burning Bridge of Friendship

How we could never forget the day we thought we were friends.

The day you held my hand and told me you'd stay.

But you lied.

Did you ever think to call? Did you ever think to ask how I'm feeling?

I'm strong and I'm here for you, yes, but I need someone to take into consideration that I'm a person too.

How I thought of our friendship was treasured, by not just me but you also.

The moments we spent day after day, hours upon hours.

But you lied.

Did you ever think of giving a remembrance of our friendship? Did you think before cutting me out of the picture?

I'm strong and I'm here for you, yes, but I need someone to take into consideration that I'm a person too.

How we admired one another's ambitions and inspired one another to go further.

The days we imagined how we'd change the world someday.

But you lied.

Did you ever think to still do those things or are they childish? Did you ever think that I wouldn't want our friendship to just be for now, but for the future?

Of course, I'll never shed a tear, never cry, but on the inside, my heart was breaking when you never thought of me and how I felt, never thought to call me first once in a while. It doesn't take much, just a little of your time. Just a little thing to show that you are still thinking of me. That I'm still on your mind. All I can do now is thank you for the second stab. Maybe this time the bruise won't heal and I will forever remember why trust is such a hard thing to give in this world because it's a gift that is earned not just taken lightly and given to anyone.

Haters are Going to Hate

They'll pull you in a million different ways to make you compromise so that they'll like you.

Until you realize that haters are going to hate whether you like it or not.

But at least you don't have to take them with you in the afterlife to judge you.

You'll purposely make a fool of yourself, purposely harm yourself in so many ways.

Until you realize that haters are going to hate whether you like it or not.

But at least you don't have to take them with you in the afterlife to judge you.

You're unique, stand out from the other stones like a buried treasure that shines when uncovered.

Until you realize that haters are going to hate whether you like it or not.

But at least you don't have to take them with you in the afterlife to judge you.

They are going to have you run circles in circles, miles upon miles so you will no longer breathe for the race.

Until you realize that haters are going to hate whether you like it or not.

But at least you don't have to take them with you in the afterlife to judge you.

Instinctively it feels good to have a crowd around you, but spiritually it's as toxic as radiation.

Until you realize that haters are going to hate whether you like it or not.

But at least you don't have to take them with you in the afterlife to judge you.

Those grimaces that they call smiles, those balled fists they call hands to shake, all lies.

Until you realize that haters are going to hate whether you like it or not.

But at least you don't have to take them with you in the afterlife to judge you.

They weren't there when you got locked up, but they call you cool, they weren't there when you got beat up and yet they call you tough.

Until you realize that haters are going to hate whether you like it or not.

But at least you don't have to take them with you in the afterlife to judge you.

Time wastes for nobody, either you're going to be there or you're not but chasing them around is not an option.

Until you realize that haters are going to hate whether you like it or not.

But at least you don't have to take them with you in the afterlife to judge you.

In this game of cat and mouse, the mouse gets cheese, the cat gets the mouse and that mouse thought it was getting something with that golden piece of cheese.

Until you realize that haters are going to hate whether you like it or not.

But at least you don't have to take them with you in the afterlife to judge you.

They'll have you burn down the house until there is nothing left, have you shoot down yourself.

Until you realize that haters are going to hate whether you like it or not.

But at least you don't have to take them with you in the afterlife to judge you.

Friends, what are they really, cowards that run away when you have problems and stick around to get you in trouble.

Until you realize that haters are going to hate whether you like it or not.

But at least you don't have to take them with you in the afterlife to judge you.

Trapped as Children, Frozen in Time

Section 5

Given Everything, You Want

Except for...

Give me that car and I shall be satisfied.

Yea, give me that car and I shall be satisfied.

Give me drink and I shall be satisfied.

Yea, give me a drink and I shall be satisfied.

Give me those mansions and I shall be satisfied.

Yea, give me those mansions and I shall be satisfied.

Give me meat and I shall be satisfied.

Yea, give me meat and I shall be satisfied.

Give me everything, then shall you be my friend.

And his parents gave him everything he asked for, but was he satisfied? Was he content? Or was he happy? No, for he had been given everything his heart desired. Except for love, attention, correction, and most of all, teaching him about God.

Note: You may think your child is happy just because you give him or her everything, but that is not so. Most children think that they want more things, but even as they grow up they still feel as if something is missing that they just don't know. Here is something that will shine a light so you'll understand your child and your child will understand the way you feel. The Bible is what shines a light on everything and everyone, and it will give the empathy you all need for each other.

They Think They Know

They think they know how to cross the street.

They think they know, but they don't.

They think because they are big and tall that they know something.

They think they know, but they don't.

They are like overgrown babies on the inside.

They think they know, but they don't.

They are a danger unto themselves and you.

They think they know, but they don't.

Eyes they have, but they don't see. Ears they have, but they don't hear.

They sometimes frustrate me, but then I remember that they are just babes on the inside.

Anger and madness have they caused me, but deep inside I love them.

Because I know that they don't know what they don't know.

Note: Many people think they know something because they are all grown up on the outside, but on the inside, they are still babies. So, do they really know?

Born to Be

I was born to be the chosen one.

I was born to be a traitor.

Born to be something good or bad is not our choice.

I was born to be kind and gentle.

I was born to be mean and horrible.

Sometimes we are born just to build up someone and tear them down.

I was born, to be honest, and truthful.

I was born to be a liar and conniving.

Born to be an honest person or a liar is not our choice, but it doesn't mean you have to stay that way.

    I was born to be me and I'm not trying to make anyone like me.

    I was born to be myself, whether you like me or not.

    Note: Born to be someone is not our choice, but God's choice. We didn't plan on being on this Earth and we can't decide our purpose on this earth either, but we can ask God to make us better or different.

Forgive You

I'm the one being beaten by your rod, welded by your fire.

And you have the nerve enough to say I forgive you?

Tell me how your mind actually works, because you were in the wrong.

I'm the one taking the arrows for everyone, being shot at when I'm not the target.

And you have the nerve enough to say I forgive you?

Tell me how your mind actually works, because you were in the wrong.

I'm the one that you smack every time something goes wrong, the one you vent on.

And you have the nerve enough to say I forgive you?

Tell me how your mind actually works, because you were in the wrong.

I'm the one you always asked to help you because you were too scared to do it yourself.

And you have the nerve enough to say I forgive you?

Tell me how your mind actually works, because you were in the wrong.

I'm the wall with a drill aimed at my head once I walk through those doors, because of what you've said.

And you have the nerve enough to say I forgive you?

Tell me how your mind actually works, because you were in the wrong.

I'm the one that has to waddle in filth that isn't even mine, but you think you're too clean to get dirty when it's your mess.

And you have the nerve enough to say I forgive you?

Tell me how your mind actually works, because you were in the wrong.

I'm the one that is always expected to take more because people forget I'm human and not an android.

And you have the nerve enough to say I forgive you?

Tell me how your mind actually works, because you were in the wrong.

I'm the one that has to put up with all the silliness you bring to the table and then when something goes wrong and I break you have the nerve enough to say I forgive you as if I've done something wrong.

Oh Child of Man

I work hard, you grow jealous.

I take care of you, you fuss.

No matter what I do, I can't help them.

I teach things, you don't hear.

I show miracles, you don't believe.

No matter what I do I can't help them.

I bring gifts, you are angered.

I celebrate, you destroy it.

No matter what I do I can't help them.

I show patience, you break me low.

I love and show charity, you hate me.

No matter what I do I can't help them.

The rain shall fall and the sun shall cease.

I cry for help, you crush me.

I save lives, you kill me.

No matter what I do I can't help them.

The rain shall fall and the sun shall cease.

Oh, child of man, oh child of man, why do you break my heart.

Cracking of thunder, flashing of lights, all fall upon me like hail.

I scream those names to stop, you do not hearken.

I plant new life, you trample it asunder.

No matter what I do I can't help them.

The rain shall fall and the sun shall cease.

Oh, child of man, oh child of man, why do you break my heart.

Cracking of thunder, flashing of lights, all fall upon me like hail.

I hold on tight, you cut me loose.

I share the hope, you pluck it out.

No matter what I do I can't help them.

Oh, child of man, oh child of man, why do you

break my heart.

Cracking of thunder, flashing of lights, all fall upon me like hail.

I ask for a hand, you slap me in the face.

I fly the dreams, you shatter them like glass.

No matter what I do I can't help them.

Oh, child of man, oh child of man, why do you break my heart.

Cracking of thunder, flashing of lights, all fall upon me like hail.

Save the children. Save the innocent. Save the blinded. If there is one good thing in you.

For my life with you has been nothing and nothing for me shall come from you, ever.

Trial By Fire, Test of Courage

Section 6

Lost

I know not who to trust, who is right, who is wrong.

For I am lost.

Time after time doing the wrong thing trying to do right.

For I am lost.

Seeing so many horrible things from the person that says they are right.

For I am lost.

I have been hurt, I have been burned so many times.

For I am lost.

Confused and tricked so many times, for so many years.

For I am lost.

Who is there to believe? Who is wrong? Am I wrong?

For I am lost.

Running in circles trying to find my way.

For I am lost.

But there seems to be no way out.

For I am lost.

The path has darkened and there is no way out.

For I am lost.

In the shadows of darkness, there is no one in sight.

For I am lost.

My heart has sunk, my mind is enraged.

For I am lost.

I feel trapped inside an invisible cage.

For I am lost.

Not knowing which path to take to lead me back.

For I am lost.

I feel that if I choose a path it may be wrong.

For I am lost.

How do I know? How will I find my way?

I cry. I weep, for I am lost. Who is there to trust? Who is there to believe? Oh did the Lord God create someone so special? Did he create someone that great to put you on the right path? Someone, please give me an answer.

"Do not weep my child, for it is I Jesus Christ, I will put you on the right path, then the truth shall reveal itself and ye shall have no doubts of rights or wrongs. For I shall guide thee down the path of truth."

Note: Sometimes we feel very lost in our hearts and we know not who is right or who is wrong. When you feel like this just read the Bible and you will hear Jesus leading you to all truth.

Time of Loneliness

Everything seems to vanish and disappear.

This is a time of loneliness.

Deep fear and anguish come about me.

This is a time of loneliness.

Voices laughing and carrying on in my head.

This is a time of loneliness.

There may be people, but we can't relate.

This is a time of loneliness.

The feeling of loneliness is as if you have been exiled from everyone.

This is a time of loneliness.

I am frustrated and upset, but there is no one to comfort me.

This is a time of loneliness.

Great darkness and shadows surround me.

Oh, who can help me? Oh, is there such a one?

Then a voice called out, saying.

"Come up and talk within me, for ye are not alone."

Then I answered and said, "Who sayeth so?"

Then the voice spoke unto me again, saying.

"It is I Christ Jesus, whom ye hath to fear not. For I am always by thy side. When everyone and everything seems to disappear. There am I in the midst of you. Now come with me and talk with me, for I will make everything alright."

Note: When you feel all alone and by yourself in the world, take your Bible or you can just talk to Him. Praying and talking. For he hears you.

The Shadow that Follows

What is it that I see, who are you that follows me?

There's a shadow that follows.

What do you want, why do you oppress me?

There's a shadow that follows.

It is dark and dreary, it only brings the past to haunt

Each time something bad happens a shadow low.

I see your face in the mirror, who are you?

There's a shadow that you see each time you look in the mirror

Remembering that which you have lost or that which has happened.

There's a shadow that follows.

It wails with the sorrow of its heart, bringing you to hurt inside.

There's a shadow that follows.

It follows you, making it so you can't forget.

There's a shadow that follows.

Too afraid to face the shadows mirror and face the hurt you carry.

There's a shadow that follows.

Each time you see the mirror, you see the shadow

There's a shadow that follows.

You walk through a dark and shadowy hall, wondering.

There's a shadow that follows

There is no one to help, you are alone and the shadow follows.

There's a shadow that follows.

The shadow has a grip on you and will not let go.

There's a shadow that follows.

There's an illusion ahead of you that shows the ones you lost and the things you lost.

There's a shadow that follows.

The shadow plays on your mind and this is no game.

There's a shadow that follows.

The more you fear the stronger it gets.

There's a shadow that follows.

Faraway your house sits and you wish you could return.

There's a shadow that follows.

You want it to stop, you want it to go away.

There's a shadow that follows.

You are broken and have fallen upon your knees.

There's a shadow that follows.

There's no light, only darkness.

You fight to stand up.

"Stand up and fight this," a voice says.

You stand but are shaken with fear. The shadow fights you and tries to get a better hold. Then when there seems to be no sign of any hope, then you see a you are on your knees, but you stand strong. It's a fight between you and your shadow to gain control again. For the shadow is not willing to give up. "Look into the mirror, face this shadow and ye shall be set free." You stand and turn towards the mirror, tears pouring from your eyes, for you do not want to face this shadow. "Face it, face your shadow." You look into that mirror and see the shadow. "Oh Lord Jesus help me, you cry

The shadow shrieks. "No, you can not, you can't."

You enter the mirror facing the shadowy memories of the past, it hurts and it is painful. Let this memory go and you shall be set free, break this mirror that traps you. I can't, yes you can, only you can set yourself free from this shadow." Then when there seems to be no way out, you see a Bible. You open the Bible and read it, the shadow covers its head and the mirror starts to crack.

"No," says the shadow, "you can't do this, stop it I say".

You pray, even more, the shadow begins to disappear and the mirror starts to shatter. "It is finished, you have broken the shadows you had created." The shadow shrieks in anger then disappears. The darkness around you clears and you return, happy as ever and Jesus right with you.

Note: Sometimes our feelings for someone or something that we have lost, create dark shadows, which are almost impossible to get rid of. Each day you see the mirror and see what tragic thing has happened

and the which you have created only gets worse. There is only one way to get rid of those shadows and that is to read God's word and face the mirror and the shadow.

Loner

My path is empty as an empty casing

For I am a loner.

But somewhere in my heart I know there are paths full.

My laugh is faint and my smile is dim like a lonely forest.

For I am a loner.

But somewhere in my heart, my laugh is not faint and my smile shines.

There is no one there for me, I am like a piece of wheat alone.

For I am a loner.

But somewhere in my heart, there is always someone there for me.

My hopes are sometimes crushed, sometimes shattered like a mirror.

For I am a loner.

But somewhere in my heart the hope lives on and grows like a tree.

My life sometimes seems to vanish in sorrow and misery like a storm.

For I am a loner.

But somewhere in my heart my life still lives though the storms carry on.

My heart sometimes sunken and breaks like a ship that has sunk.

For I am a loner.

But somewhere in my heart it can not sink or be broken.

My light sometimes seems like it can no longer shine, like a star with no life.

For I am a loner.

My mind is sometimes confused like a person lost at the crossing of paths.

For I am a loner.

But somewhere in my heart the light still shines and glows.

But somewhere in my heart I know the truth and am not confused.

My eyes sometimes shed tears of disappointment like a river of sorrow.

My dreams and prayers sometimes seem to be taken away like grass in a storm.

For I am a loner.

But somewhere in my heart the dreams and prayers still live on and continue.

My feeling and emotions sometimes crushed by others like a stone and heart

For I am a loner.

But somewhere in my heart my feelings and emotions are not crushed.

For I am a loner.

But somewhere in my heart, there is no disappointment or tears.

My step is alone for no one walks with me, for I am like a bird flying alone.

For I am a loner.

But somewhere in my heart,t someone walks with me.

My story is one that is sometimes lonely, sometimes disappointing, sometimes broken for

am a loner, but though I am a loner my heart is never alone and in my heart is where I live and

I am no longer a loner.

Note: Through everything in life that you've been through all the lonely times, your heart is

what always got you through it, because in your heart dwells Jesus and Jesus is sometimes

the only one to strengthen you. Jesus kept those dreams living, kept those prayers answered,

although these things sometimes take time and perseverance. Till those dreams and prayers

are answered he will keep that light shining and keep that heart going until you get there, no

matter what. Although your path is sometimes empty, sometimes lonely, Jesus is in your heart to tell you to keep going and keep reaching forth to the prize, he has promised you. Although there are sometimes disappointments, sometimes crushed feelings and emotions, Jesus is there in your heart to heal that and to take those crushed feelings away. Although your heart feels sometimes broken, sometimes shattered into pieces, Jesus is there in your heart so that it can not be broken or shattered. Although sometimes your laugh is faint and sometimes your smile dim, Jesus is still inside living in you and your laugh is no longer faint and your smile no longer dim. Although there Sometimes times of confusion and misdirection on the inside, Jesus is still there to make sure that you are not turned the wrong way and is there to guide you to the turn. Although sometimes your light may seem not to shine anymore, Jesus is still there and the light will shine as long as he's there. The heart is the place where Jesus will guide and help us all as long as we believe and trust in him, no matter how lonely we get in this world.

Love and Departure

Section 7

Together Forever and Ever

Together we took vows stating that we are together forever.

Together we go through trials and tribulation.

Together we sing and dance.

Together we promised we would always be there for one another.

Together we share tears and weeping.

Together we knew that we were created for one another.

Together there is nothing that can stand in our way.

Together we eat and together we cook.

Together we enjoy each other's company and companionship.

Together we were created and made.

Together we said that no matter what happens to each of us good or bad we would always be there.

Together we share love and happiness with one another.

Together we said there is no other person made for like you.

Together we share our youth and together we share our old age.

We will be together forever and ever, Amen and Amen.

Note: Do you know what a real wedding is? A real wedding is when you take those vows and say that you will take this man to be your husband, and when the man says that he will take this woman to be his wife. When you say that you are tied together forever and ever and let no storm too strong, let no wind too swift take that away from you.

Illusion

That this moment isn't just a dream, that you aren't with me.

Say it isn't so, say that you love me.

And that the magic won't fade till 12 o'clock giving us time to dance in our illusion.

That these tears I shed aren't for you, that you aren't feeling what I'm feeling.

Say it isn't so, say that you love me.

And that the magic won't fade till 12 o'clock giving us time to dance in our illusion.

That you are going to leave me now, that all of this was just an illusion.

Say it isn't so, say that you love me.

And that the magic won't fade till 12
o'clock giving us time to dance in our illusion.
That your hand is slipping away from mine,
that you are not the one.
Say it isn't so, say that you love me.
And that the magic won't fade till 12
o'clock giving us time to dance in our illusion.
That you never cared in the first place,
that you never saw anything.
Say it isn't so, say that you love me.
And that the magic won't fade till 12
o'clock giving us time to dance in our illusion.
That I only wished it to be so, that I
wanted to be something else.
Say it isn't so, say that you love me.
And that the magic won't fade till 12
o'clock giving us time to dance in our illusion.

That you're enjoying the misery I'm in, that you can go on about your day.

Say it isn't so, say that you love me.

And that the magic won't fade till 12 o'clock giving us time to dance in our illusion.

That you were fading away from me long ago, that you were becoming a ghost.

Say it isn't so, say that you love me.

And that the magic won't fade till 12 o'clock giving us time to dance in our illusion.

That everything we felt was just a bunch of dreams, that none of it was real.

Say it isn't so, say that you love me.

And that the magic won't fade till 12 o'clock giving us time to dance in our illusion.

That the magic is fading, that we are starting to vanish from one another's reach.

Say it isn't so, say that you love me.

And that the magic won't fade till 12 o'clock giving us time to dance in our illusion.

That this isn't real, that this was something we both wanted to be true and isn't.

Say it isn't so, say that you love me.

And we can continue our illusion that only lives in our minds and that the magic won't fade till 12 o'clock giving us time to dance and make merry in our illusion while we still have it.

Before This

The length of time couldn't be measured as the hair upon our heads.

Before this, we were together and of one soul.

And then the ground quaked and we were separated by the great fault that left us reaching for one another's hand, but the gap is even further than the strength of our bond.

There wasn't such a thing as a past, present, or future we were just here in existence.

Before this, we were together and of one soul.

And then we fell, slipped off the edge like all those before us into an endless sea.

There wasn't such a thing as lost and found or even a two-way path.

Before this, we were together and of one soul.

And then the sky opened and swallowed the world as we knew it with its mouth, for it wept that it couldn't have what the children below had.

There wasn't such a thing as being afraid of you or your thoughts.
Before this, we were together and of one soul.
And then the tails of that serpent wrapped around you and dragged you away from my grasp.
There wasn't such a thing as loneliness or depression because I had you then.
Before this, we were together and of one soul.
And then like a flash of lightning we were both struck with tears at birth and no one knows why except for us, for in those first few moments we remember what we lost and what is to come.
There wasn't such a thing as words to tell what was on your mind for we were one.
Before this, we were together and of one soul.
And then when we reached this Earth our souls visited that graveyard where we buried the one we lost in eternity.

In Memory

I can watch us run along the brooks of Keydron.

Although it is not so now.

But in memory, I can always return and relive those moments with you, those moments I have now lost.

I can hear our laughter when we were once friends and family.

Although it is not so now.

But in memory, I can always return and relive those moments with you, those moments I have now lost.

I can only imagine some of the things I wish I had then was here now.

Although it is not so now.

But in memory, I can always return and relive those moments with you, those moments I have now lost.

I can embrace the times we watched the stars sparkle like a scattered barrel of diamonds.

Although it is not so now.

But in memory, I can always return and relive those moments with you, those moments I have now lost.

I can dream of when we shared those special moments without words and just silence.

Although it is not so now.

But in memory, I can always return and relive those moments with you, those moments I have now lost.

I can always be the child that I no longer am; full of imagination and innocence.

Although it is not so now.

But in memory, I can always return and relive those moments with you, those moments I have now lost.

I can always remember the times I fell and you were there to wipe away my tears and told me to keep on running.

Although it is not so now.

But in memory, I can always return and relive those moments with you, those moments I have now lost.

I can always retell the stories we once told our parents as children.

Although it is not so now.

But in memory, I can always return and relive those moments with you, those moments I have now lost.

I can always remember your youthful face, no matter your age now.

Although it is not so now.

But in memory, I can always return and relive those moments with you, those moments I have now lost.

I can always recall the times when you were there to stop me from doing the unthinkable and made me remember that people do care and love me.

Although it is not so now.

But in memory, I can always return and relive those moments with you, those moments I have now lost.

I can always believe that you will be with me no matter where the currents take you, no matter how life turns and makes us go our separate ways.

Although it is not so now.

But in memory I can always return and relive those moments with you, those moments I have now lost and it is there that we will always be together forever and ever till someday we return home and are able to do the things as we did as children once again.

Mirage Du Crépuscule

A figure of clear air racing into the forest only to appear and vanish before mine eyes.

Mirage du crépuscule, where hath thou gone to where I cannot find you?

And how can this be, when you were me and I were you and yet I lost you again?

A hand that fadeth right through mine, when I reach for your hand.

Mirage du crépuscule, where hath thou gone to where I cannot find you?

And how can this be, when you were me and I were you and yet I lost you again?

A shadow stabbing me through my heart and I die before your eyes for you have returned but you were too late.

Mirage du crépuscule, where hath thou gone to where I cannot find you?

And how can this be, when you were me and I were you and yet I lost you again?

A time when we both were just the atmosphere, not even a part of this capsule of sadness.

Mirage du crépuscule, where hath thou gone to where I cannot find you?

And how can this be, when you were me and I were you and yet I lost you again?

A long time ago your spirit and mine were kin, but here we are pin without memory of another.

Mirage du crépuscule, where hath thou gone to where I cannot find you?

And how can this be, when you were me and I were you and yet I lost you again?

A look into a mirror, a flash of what we used to be whenever we touch it but cannot feel the touch of another's hand.

Mirage du crépuscule, where hath thou gone to where I cannot find you?

And how can this be, when you were me and I were you and yet I lost you again?

A look into your eyes, a look into mine and we know, but we don't know what we know.

Mirage du crépuscule, where hath thou gone to where I cannot find you?

And how can this be, when you were me and I were you and yet I lost you again?

A mind that cracks into insanity, a heart that breaks like the strings of the harp that David once held.

Mirage du crépuscule, where hath thou gone to where I cannot find you?

And how can this be, when you were me and I were you and yet I lost you again?

A fear that is so great we're blinded, a turbulence so strong we're pulled apart.

Mirage du crépuscule, where hath thou gone to where I cannot find you?

And how can this be, when you were me and I were you and yet I lost you again?

A glimpse of your cloak and I know who you are, but I do not know if you are the dark rider that stabbed my heart long ago.

Mirage du crépuscule, where hath thou gone to where I cannot find you?

And how can this be, when you were me and I were you and yet I lost you again?

A lake that stares back, but cannot speak for it has no mouth so it rushes against the stones to roar with fury of the ones who fell victim to his anger.

Mirage du crépuscule, where hath thou gone to where I cannot find you?

And how can this be, when you were me and I were you and yet I lost you again?

A voice that whispers into our ears and tells us, but we're convinced it is only a trap of sin.

Mirage du crépuscule, where hath thou gone to where I cannot find you?

And how can this be, when you were me and I were you and yet I lost you again?

A lie that sprouts from their mouths and into a fire that seeks to burn us alive.

Mirage du crépuscule, where hath thou gone to where I cannot find you?

And how can this be, when you were me and I were you and yet I lost you again?

A breath that hurts to take for my heart is overtaken by the arrows that stung it.

Mirage du crépuscule, where hath thou gone to where I cannot find you?

And how can this be, when you were me and I were you and yet I lost you again?

A pain that can be quenched to make me smile even in death when you were here.

Mirage du crépuscule, where hath thou gone to where I cannot find you?

And how can this be, when you were me and I were you and yet I lost you again?

A lifetime compared to days is no match, although it is yet just a half glass.

Mirage du crépuscule, where hath thou gone to where I cannot find you?

And how can this be, when you were me and I were you and yet I lost you again?

A grin on lonlinesses face when he is moved by the prison I have been thrown away to without a cause.

Mirage du crépuscule, where hath thou gone to where I cannot find you?

And how can this be, when you were me and I were you and yet I lost you again?

A tree in a desert that turns out to be more sand and just a glimpse of what this heart ached for most.

Mirage du crépuscule, where hath thou gone to where I cannot find you?

And how can this be, when you were me and I were you and yet I lost you again?

A figure that taps me on the shoulder, but when I turn I only see that shattered glass.

Mirage du crépuscule, where hath thou gone to where I cannot find you?

And how can this be, when you were me and I were you and yet I lost you again?

Chagrin d' Amour

An hourglass can't count the time that I feel on the inside.

Chagrin d'Amour.

My heart is breaking without you petit rose for I can no longer bear this crown without you.

Weight is like shame, fate is without fame and I feel my legs tremble with every step.

Chagrin d'Amour.

My heart is breaking without you petit rose for I can no longer bear this crown without you.

Pain has almost become a part of life, but the sting of thorns without the soothing of the rose is like complete distress, like part of me has been cut off and the other still strives to survive.

Chagrin d' Amour.

My heart is breaking without you petit rose for I can no longer bear this crown without you.

I can see thy phantom, but I cannot reach thee for ye have forgotten me.

Chagrin d'Amour.

My heart is breaking without you petit rose for I can no longer bear this crown without you.

Coldness from thy heart feels as if ye have completely abandoned me to join the other flowers.

Chagrin d'Amour.

My heart is breaking without you petit rose for I can no longer bear this crown without you.

Ye join them upon that little boat on that cold river to sail away from me so I will no longer exist to thee, though ye know I do.

Chagrin d'Amour.

My heart is breaking without you petit rose for I can no longer bear this crown without you.

It ades me. It bades me to watch ye sink below while I freeze above on this desolate island of eternal winter and night.

Chagrin d'Amour.

My heart is breaking without you petit rose for I can no longer bear this crown without you.

Can't speak to you for you shall turn your head and not hear me, can't feel you for you've thrown the key far away so I cannot unlock the door to help you remember.

Chagrin d'Amour.

My heart is breaking without you petit rose for I can no longer bear this crown without you.

Arrows have struck my heart that it shall never heal but bleed till death do it's part.

Chagrin d'Amour.

My heart is breaking without you petit rose for I can no longer bear this crown without you.

Surely you shall see the tears in mine eyes, the pain in my heart so I can only feel this life perish away from me.

Chagrin d'Amour.

My heart is breaking without you petit rose for I can no longer bear this crown without you.

Your heart shall be pierced and shall wail to see how you have abandoned your first love for the world.

Chagrin d'Amour.

My heart is breaking without you petit rose for I can no longer bear this crown without you.

How shalt thou bring me back to you and save me from the blood that rains down my head from beneath this crown?

Chagrin d'Amour.

My heart is breaking without you petit rose for I can no longer bear this crown without you.

Remember the time we first found another in paradise, remember when ye were a part of me and I, a part of thee to make one?

Chagrin d'Amour.

My heart is breaking without you petit rose for I can no longer bear this crown without you.

If thou shalt not remember me, then how shall I remember what it is to live, to love, to fight, to hold thy hand once more?

Chagrin d'Amour.

My heart is breaking without you petit rose for I can no longer bear this crown without you.

If I shall perish, I shall perish for thee petit rose and in thy remembrance so that I shall live on, but if thou forgettest me then I shall perish in vain and all this shall be as in vein also.

Chagrin d'Amour.

My heart is breaking without you petit rose for I can no longer bear this crown without you.

Remember the marriage we had prepared or haste thou forgotten that for the fantasies of this world.

Chagrin d'Amour.

My heart is breaking without you petit rose for I can no longer bear this crown without you.

Promises are meant to be made, but not broken as a token that is given and taken away.

Chagrin d'Amour.

My heart is breaking without you petit rose for I can no longer bear this crown without you.

Thou was deceived for that one who pretended to be me, but do I not have that feeling that we both share, do I not bear the signature in mine eyes that I am yours and you are mine.

Chagrin d'Amour.

My heart is breaking without you petit rose for I can no longer bear this crown without you.

Now that you have forgotten me I shall perish away for a little while from thee for my words are as dead unto you and for your love means nothing compared to what you see in this oasis that shall soon be covered by night and snow.

Chagrin d'Amour.

My heart is breaking without you petit rose for I can no longer bear this crown without you.

Someday you shall remember me and weep that ye had left me for this once you see how real this is compared to what we had and you shall return to the place we first met, but I shall not be there not for a long, long time, but someday I will come back for you.

                      Chagrin d'Amour.

    My heart is breaking without you petit rose for I can no longer bear this crown without you.

    For though thou turnest thy back from me, I have not turned my back from thee and thy weeping, but as of now, ye shall slumber petit rose until I return to awaken thee from thy long slumber so that we shall be wed and bring heaven upon this world so that all evil shall perish and our kingdom established.

                      Chagrin d'Amour.

    My heart is breaking without you petit rose for I can no longer bear this crown without you.

    Remember my voice, remember my signature, remember that I am thy one and only love.

                      Chagrin d'Amour.

    My heart is breaking without you petit rose for I can no longer bear this crown without you.

    As for now, I kiss thee goodnight and even in thy night, my spirit you shall always remember in thy long dream for part of me shall always still be there to guide thee and help you remember me and that ye only have so long before I come to save thee from that dragon.

Chagrin d'Amour.

My heart is breaking without thee, petit rose for I can no longer bear this crown without you, but I will be able to come back for you and ye shall know the next time that I am the one you are bewedded to and that dragon shall be slain before the foot of the cross.

www.ingramcontent.com/pod-product-compliance
Lightning Source LLC
Chambersburg PA
CBHW062036290426
44109CB00026B/2642